Discover
Seychelles Creole Cuisine

Introduction to Seychelles Creole Cuisine

The Seychelles Creole Cuisine, as we know it today, owes its origin to the island nation's first settlers who were of French, Indian, African and later, Chinese descent.

Although ruled for the longest period of time by the United Kingdom, the British failed to leave any impression on the taste buds of the islanders.

Over the years, the Seychellois creole cuisine has evolved and today, characterised by unique flavours, fragrances, tastes and varying degrees of spiciness, it has claimed its unique place in the culinary world.

Unquestionably, the abundant use of fresh herbs in our cooking is due to the French influence. The Indians brought in exotic blends of spices while traditional methods of preparing fruits and root vegetables or 'gro manze' available locally, were taught to us by our African forebears.

The seas around The Seychelles are rich in hundreds of species of some of the tastiest fishes on the planet and this is why fish

Seychellois grow in their home gardens many of the fresh ingredients that go into some of the dishes and readily share these with neighbours and friends. Around most homes, you will see growing papaya, curry leaves, moringa spinach, chillies, limes, herbs and even bananas. Harvested just prior to cooking these are all very important to the Seychelles cuisine.

The Seychellois way of preparing curries, stews, broths and grilled fish is unique. Visitors often frown when they learn that we cook our chicken curry with bone in or

is central to the Seychellois family meals. When fish is scarce during the South-East monsoons, there are lots of unhappy families.

The Seychelles vegetation is lush and verdant. Coconut plantations once covered large swathes of the coastal plains and amongst the greenery you can still find the coconut palm growing in large numbers. No part of the palm goes to waste and from the nut we extract the fresh coconut milk that is used in many of our dishes.

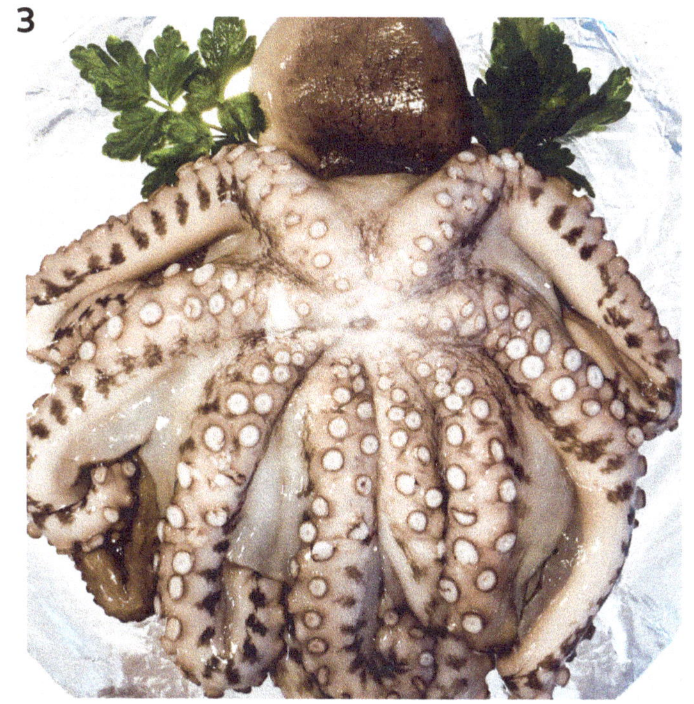

that we prefer our fish grilled whole rather than in fillet.

The manner in which spices and condiments are used in Seychelles creole cuisine reflect the ethnic diversity and origins of its people. The blend of spices is the base for some mouth-watering and exotic cooking.

The basic ingredients of the Seychelles cuisine are:

*   tomatoes - ponm d'amour
*   onions - zonyon
*   root ginger - zenzam

4

*   garlic - lay
*   chillies - piman
*   thyme - diten
*   parsley – persi
*   curry leaves – karipile
*   coconut milk – dile koko
*   curry powder –masala
*   turmeric – safran

Bought directly from the fishermen when the catch comes in or from the market bottom line fishes such as snappers, groupers, are firm favourites amongst locals. Other delicacies such as lobsters

About four decades ago, meat was to be found on the family table on only Sundays due to their high prices. With now higher disposable income, families can enjoy their chicken stew or pork curry, prepared in the unique creole way any day of the week.

A whole fish prepared in a marinade of crushed chillies, ginger and garlic, onions and herbs, and then grilled, is the showpiece at family celebrations and gatherings. Even hotel resorts have adopted this classic dish when they feature creole buffet nights at their establishments.

and crabs are also found but these are mainly seasonal and in the case of lobster in open season only.

Demersal fish species loved by locals are trevallies of all types, tuna, bonito, dorado and wahoo.

Coconut milk is widely used in curries and desserts and is most often squeezed fresh from the grated nuts just before cooking starts. Octopus cooked in coconut milk is one of the most exquisite seafood dishes you can feast on and is revered by locals.

A Seychellois meal would be incomplete without accompaniments such as chutneys and salads prepared in myriads of ways from golden apple, mango, papaya, pumpkin and aubergine.

This book is intended to take you on a journey of discovery of the creole cuisine of the Seychelles based on recipes and methods exactly as we use in our homes. It is also a 'pictorial essay' of the Seychelles and we hope it whets your appetite in more ways than one.

Happy cooking.

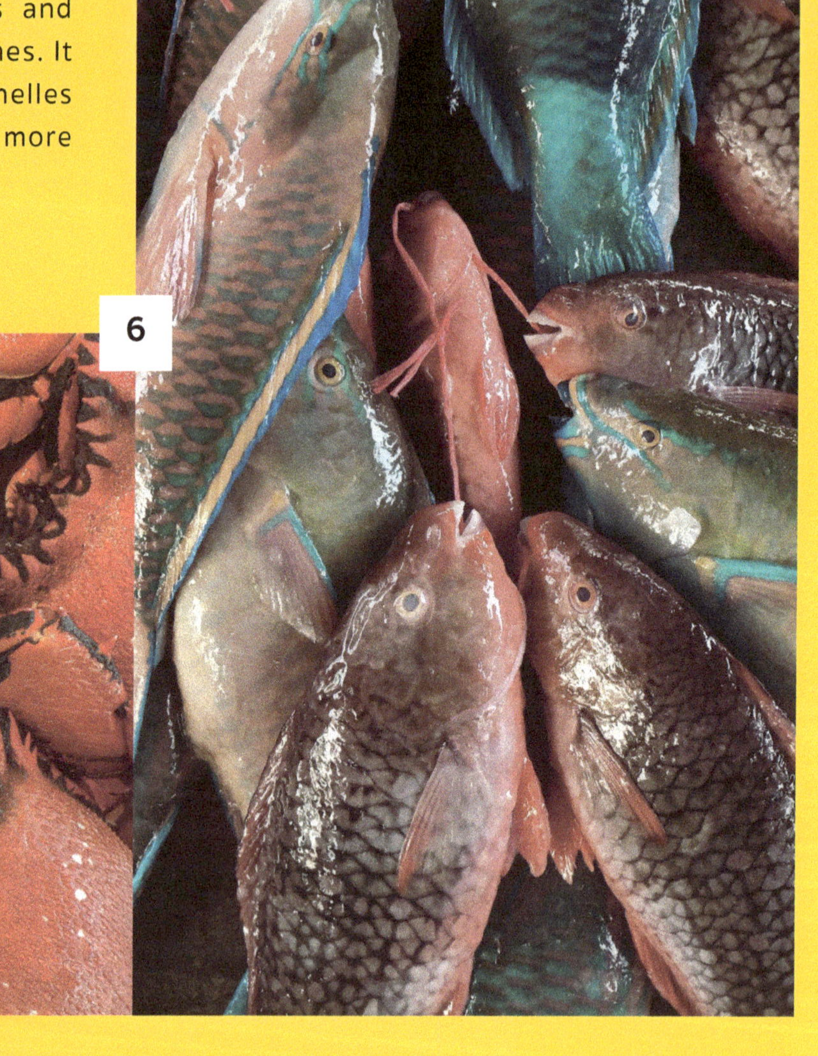

"Coco de Mer (Lodoicea Maldivica) The World's largest seed."

Table of Contents

condiments & snacks

desserts

Aubergine Chutney (Satini Brinzel)

Ingredients

- 1 kg **aubergine**
- 2 **medium onions** finely sliced
- **Chillies**, washed and ground
  (quantity to your liking)
- 3 tbsp **sunflower oil**
- 3 tsp **vinegar or lime**
- **Salt and pepper**
- Chopped **spring onion** for garnish

Method

1. Wash the aubergine, remove the stalk and cut into big pieces
2. Boil the aubergine pieces in a big pan until soft
3. Drain and when cool, scoop out flesh and discard the skin
4. Mash the flesh well using a fork
5. In a large bowl, mix the mashed aubergine and the sliced onion
6. Add the oil, a spoon at time and beat the mixture using a whisk or fork
7. Add vinegar or lime
8. Season with salt and pepper
9. Arrange in a serving dish and garnish with spring onions.

Avocado Salad (Salad Zavoka)

Ingredients

- 2 large **avocadoes**
- Juice from 2 **limes or lemons**
- 3 tablespoons light **olive oil or sunflower oil**
- 1 small **brown onion**, finely diced
- 1 half teaspoon of **salt**
- Pinch of **ground black pepper**

Method

1. Peel the avocadoes, cut into half, discard the stones and slice into 1 cm slices
2. Arrange the avocado slices in a serving dish
3. Make a vinaigrette from the oil, lime juice, diced onions, salt and pepper – sugar (optional) may also be added
4. Pour the vinaigrette evenly over the sliced avocados and place in the refrigerator for at least 10 minutes before serving.

Bitter Melon Salad (Salad Margoz)

Ingredients

- 2 medium size **bitter melon** (approx. 500 grammes)
- 1 medium size **red onion** onion finely sliced
- Dressing made from 3 tbsp of **sunflower oil**, 2 tablespoons diluted **brown vinegar**, salt and **ground pepper**
- Chopped **chillies** optional

Method

1. Remove the top and tail, cut in half length wise and remove all seeds
2. Sliced to desired thickness, preferably on the thin side
3. Soak the sliced bitter melon in boiled water for around 10 minutes
4. Drain and squeeze to remove all the water
5. In a salad bowl mix the bitter melon and sliced onions well
6. Pour the salad dressing in the bowl and mix well.
7. Arrange in serving dish
8. Note: Allow to stand in the fridge for 10 mins before serving for a refreshing effect.

Breadfruit Salad (Salad Friyapen)

Ingredients

- 1 big mature unripe **breadfruit**
- 1 medium **onion** sliced
- Juice from 2 **limes**
- 3 tablespoon **sunflower oil**
- **Salt and pepper**
- 2 teaspoons chopped **spring onions**

Method

1. Cut the breadfruit into quarters
2. Peel and remove the middle part
   and wash
3. Cook in boiling water to which has been
   added some salt (About 10 to 15 minutes
   – avoid overcooking)
4. Remove from water and drain under
   running cold water to stop the
   cooking process
5. Allow to cool down and then cut into slices
   or cubes
6. Make a vinaigrette from the oil, lime
   juice, salt and pepper
7. Mix the breadfruit and slice onions in a
   serving dish
8. Pour the vinaigrette on the breadfruit
9. Garnish with spring onions
10. Serve as a side dish.

Chokos Salad (Salad Sousout)

Ingredients

- 2 medium size **chokos**
  (approx. 250 grammes)
- 1 medium size **red onion** finely sliced
- Dressing made from 3 tbsp of **sunflower oil**,
  2 tablespoons diluted **brown vinegar,
  salt and ground pepper**
- Chopped **chillies** optional

Method

1. Peel the chokos, cut into quarters and
   remove the stone inside
2. Cut in wedges and place in a pan of boiling
   water to which has been added one
   teaspoon of bicarbonate of soda
   This makes the chokos
   retain its colour and look more presentable.
3. Boil until you can drive a pointed object all
   the water across a piece
4. Drain and allow to cool down
5. In a small bowl, mix the sliced onions and
   the dressing
6. Arrange the cooled chokos in a serving
   dish and pour and spread the onion
   dressing on top
7. Note: Allow to stand in the fridge for
   10 minutes before serving for a
   refreshing effect.

Egg, Potato and Beetroot Salad

Ingredients

- 6 **eggs**
- 6 medium size **potatoes**
- 1 medium **red onion** sliced and soaked in boiled water for 5 minute and then squeezed to remove all the water
- vinaigrette made from 2 teaspoons of diluted **brown vinegar**, 3 tablespoons of **sunflower oil, salt and pepper**
- 425g tin sliced **beetroot**

Method

1. Boil the eggs until hard boiled
2. Boil the potatoes skin on until cooked through
3. Peel and slice the eggs and potatoes lengthwise and set aside
4. Drain the sliced beetroot and set aside
5. Make a salad dressing from the vinaigrette and the onions
6. Arrange the potatoes, beetroot and eggs in a serving dish layer by layer until all used up
7. Spread the onion salad over the dish and garnish carefully
8. Place in the refrigerator for at least 10 minutes before serving.

Golden Apple Chutney (Satini Frisiter)

Ingredients

- 8 **golden apple** (approx. 1 kg)
- 1 medium size **red onion** finely sliced
- Dressing made from 2 tablespoon of **sunflower oil**, 2 tablespoons diluted **brown vinegar**, 2 tablespoons **sugar**, **salt and ground pepper**
- Chopped **chillies** optional

Method

1. Wash and peel the golden apple
2. Grate using medium perforation of a grater
3. Place in a large mixing bowl and add the rest of the ingredients and mix thoroughly
4. Adjust for seasoning to desired taste
5. Arrange in serving dish
6. Note: Allow to stand in the fridge for 10 minutes before serving for a refreshing effect.

Green Pawpaw Chutney
(Satini Papay)

Ingredients

- 1 **green pawpaw** (approx. 1 kg)
- I medium size **onion** finely sliced
- 3 **chillies** thinly chopped
- 3 tbsp of **sunflower oil**
- Juice from 2 **limes**
- **Salt and pepper** to taste
- 1 level tsp **turmeric** (optional)

Method

1. Peel the pawpaw, wash properly
2. Cut into quarters, scrape and remove all seeds
3. Grate using medium perforation
4. Soak the grated pawpaw in boiled water for around 10 minutes
5. Drain and squeeze to remove all the water
6. In a deep fry-pan, heat the oil and lightly fry the onion to soften it
7. Add the grated pawpaw to pan and stir to mix properly
8. Add the turmeric If you wish and stir until an even colour achieved
9. Add salt, pepper and chillies and keep stirring to avoid browning
10. After 5 minutes, remove from the pan, add the lime juice and mix
11. Arrange in serving dish.

25

Palm Heart Salad (Salad Palmis)

Ingredients

- 500 gms sliced **palm heart**
- ½ **brown onion** thinly sliced and soaked in cold water for 5 minutes
- 2 tablespoons **sunflower** or **vegetable oil** (do not use olive oil)
- 2 tablespoons of **white sugar**
- juice from 2 **limes** or 1 tablespoon of **white vinegar**
- dash of **salt** and **pepper**
- 1 teaspoon of finely chopped **spring onion** for garnishing
- 1 bowl of **water** in which juice of 2 additional **limes** have been squeezed

Method

1. Slice the palm heart finely and keep in the bowl of water infused with lime juice to stop the palm heart going brown while you prepare the other ingredients
2. Soak the sliced onions in cold water for 5 minutes and then remove the water
3. Make a vinaigrette from the rest of the ingredients
4. Drain the palm heart of the water and transfer to a serving dish and mix with the onions
5. Pour the vinaigrette evenly over the dish
6. Garnish with the spring onions
7. Keep in the refrigerator for at least 10 minutes, prior to serving.

Pumpkin Chutney (Satini Zironmon)

Ingredients

- 1 medium size **pumpkin**
- 1 medium size **white or brown onion**
  finely sliced
- 2 tbsp of **sunflower oil**
- juice from 2 big **limes**
  (vinegar can be used if preferred)
- **salt and ground pepper**
- chopped **chillies** (optional)
- chopped **spring onions**

Method

1. Peel the pumpkin, cut into quarters and remove the seed
2. Cut in wedges and place in a pan of boiling water
3. When cooked through, drain and allow to cool down
4. Mash with a fork or potato masher in a large bowl and mix with the sliced onion
5. Add the oil, and mix vigorously
6. Add lime juice, salt, pepper and mix again until a good consistency is obtain
7. Adjust seasoning if required
8. Garnish with chopped spring onions
9. Note: Allow to stand in the fridge for 10 mins before serving for a refreshing effect.

Shark Chutney (Satini reken)

Ingredients

- 1 kg **shark meat**
- **Onion** 1 medium – cut in fine rings
- **Garlic** 2 cloves – Finely grated
- **Ginger** – 2 cms finely grated
- 2 **Bilimbis** –preferably fresh and cut in half a centimeter rings
- **Chillis** – 6 cut in small rings with seeds
- 2 Sprigs of **thyme** finely chopped.
- Teaspoon of chopped **parsley**
- **Salt and pepper**
- 2 teaspoon **turmeric powder**
- 2 tablespoon **Sunflower Oil**
- Juice from 2 **limes or vinegar**
- Finely cut rings of **spring onions** for garnishing

Method

1. Wash the shark meat with skin on under running water
2. Cook the meat in a large saucepan of boiling water with some salt added (Cooks faster if cut into smaller pieces)
3. When the meat is cooked through, drain and place in cold water to cool it
4. Remove the skin, any dark pieces from blood and any cartilage
5. Squeeze all the water out of the meat and flake the meat into a bowl
6. To the bowl, add the onion rings, garlic, ginger, bilimbi, chillies, thyme, parsley, salt and pepper and sprinkle the turmeric on top
7. Mix thoroughly using a wooden spoon to avoid your hands getting stained
8. In a big frying pan or a wok, heat the oil
9. Add the contents of the bowl and stir until all the ingredients are properly cooked
10. The meat should be a uniform yellow colour by then
11. Remove from heat and allow to cool a little bit before adding the lime juice or some vinegar, whichever is your preference
12. Garnish with some finely cut rings of spring onions.

Snake Gourd Salad (Salad Patol)

Ingredients

- 1 medium size **snake gourd**
  (approx. 500 grammes)
- 1 medium size **red onion** onion finely sliced
- Dressing made from 3 tbsp of **sunflower oil**,
  2 tablespoons diluted **brown vinegar,**
  salt and ground pepper
- Chopped **chillies** optional

Method

1. Scrape the snake gourd until all green on the outside
2. Remove the top and tail, cut in half length wise and remove all seeds
3. Sliced to desired thickness, preferably on the thin side
4. Soak the slice snake gourd in boiled water for around 10 minutes
5. Drain and squeeze to remove all the water
6. In a salad bowl mix the snake gourd and sliced onions well
7. Pour the salad dressing in the bowl and mix well. Arrange in serving dish

Note: Allow to stand in the fridge for 10mins before serving for a refreshing effect.

White Cucumber Salad
(Salad Kokom Blan)

Ingredients

- 1 medium **white cucumber**
- 1 medium **red onion** sliced
- Dressing made from 2 tablespoon **sunflower oil**, I tablespoon diluted **brown vinegar, salt and pepper**
- 1 teaspoon **spring onions** for garnishing

Method

1. Peel the cucumber, cut in half lengthwise and de-seed

2. Slice the cumber in rings into desired thickness
3. Place the cucumber in warm salted water for minutes. May be omitted if a crunchy effect is preferred
4. Place the sliced onions in cold water for 5mins
5. Make a dressing as in ingredients above
6. Drain the cucumber, squeeze the water from it and arrange in a mixing bowl
7. Drain the onion and mix with the cucumber
8. Transfer to a serving dish and pour the dressing evenly over the cucumber/onion mix
9. Garnish with the spring onions and place in the refrigerator for at least 5 minutes before serving

soups & sides

Fish Broth Rabbit Fish/Snapper (Bouyon Blanc)

Ingredients

- 1 kilo of **white meat fish, rabbit fish, red emperor snapper**
- 1 medium **onion** sliced
- 1 medium **tomato** cubed
- 2 cloves **garlic** grated
- 3/4 inch **ginger** grated
- 3 sprigs **thyme**
- 3 tablespoon **sunflower oil**
- **salt and pepper**
- 3 **bilimbis** cut in quarters lengthways

Method

1. Clean the fish properly and cut it in pieces
2. Season with salt and pepper and set aside
3. Heat the oil in a saucepan on medium setting
4. Fry the onions, garlic and ginger to soften
5. Add the fish, tomato, bilimbis and thyme and mix gently
6. Add enough water to cover the fish pieces
7. Cover and simmer for 15 to 20 minutes or until the fish has cooked through
8. Season with salt and pepper
9. Best served with rice and freshly ground chilli sauce.

Spinach Broth (Bouyon Bred)

Amaranth, (Payater), Chinese cabbage (Soupsin),
Moringa (Mouroum), Pumpkin leaves
(Bred Zironmon)

Ingredients

- Big bunch of any the above
- 1 medium size **brown onion**, peeled
  and sliced
- 2 cloves **garlic** minced
- ½ garlic grated
- 1 tablespoon **sunflower oil**
- **Salt and ground pepper**
- Warm **water**

Method

1. Wash and cut your spinach (bred)
2. Heat the oil in saucepan, and soften the
   onions and add the spinach
3. Add the ginger and garlic and mix well
4. Add warm water, enough to just cover
   the spinach
5. Season with salt and paper
6. Reduce heat to simmer for 10 minutes
7. Remove when the spinach has just cooked
   through. Overcooking destroys the vitamins
   in the spinach
8. Allow to stand for 5 minutes before serving
9. Serve as a side dish with main course and
   preferably rice.

Trevally Fish Balls (Boulet Karang)

Ingredients

- **Karang Fillet** 1.5 kg (preferably Balo –Bludger)
- **Onion** 1 medium – diced
- **Garlic** 2 cloves – finely grated
- **Ginger** – 1 inch finely grated
- **Eggs** – 2
- **Persil** – 3 shoots finely chopped
- **Thyme** – 3 shoots finely chopped
- **Salt**
- **Pepper**
- **Flour** – half a cup
- **Oil (sunflower)** for frying

Method

You can now either do one of the following:

1. Mince the fish with a cleaver while still raw until a rough mince is obtained
2. Season with salt and pepper and boil in a small amount of water, then mince or
3. Steam it for 5 to 10 minutes, allow to cool down, then mince.

In a large bowl, mix well the minced fish with onions, grated ginger, garlic, parsley, thyme, salt and pepper. When thoroughly mixed, add the eggs and continue mixing while adding a little flour at a time until you get a good consistency

and the mixture is not too sticky.

Form the mixture into small balls using some flour to achieve a uniform round shape.

Deep fry into hot oil and when a uniform brown colour is obtained remove them and place on absorbent kitchen paper towel to drain as much oil as possible.

Best served while still hot, with rice and chutneys, or on its own with creole sauce or chilli sauce.

Plain Lentils (Lantiy)

Ingredients

- 2 cups of **red lentils**
- 2 tablespoon **sunflower oil**
- **Salt** and **ground pepper**
- **Water**

Method

1. Pour 2 cups of red lentils in a bowl and wash thoroughly
2. Transfer the lentils into a medium pan, add 4 cups of water and bring to the boil on a medium to high heat, add the oil
3. Reduce heat to medium to low and cook the lentils are until soft and creamy to your liking, stirring frequently
4. Add water as necessary
5. Add salt and pepper to taste
6. Serve as a side dish with main course and preferably rice.

Grilled Breadfruit (Friyapen Griye)

Ingredients

- Whole mature **breadfruit**
  - as many as you wish to eat
- A very hot open fire

Method

1. Make an open fire with wood, coconut husks or shells, or simply charcoal or briquettes
2. A kettle barbecue (Weber style) works well using charcoal

3. Ensure your fire is truly burning with serious flames leaping
4. Insert the breadfruit in the fire and cover as much as possible with charcoal or wood
5. After 10 minutes, turn the breadfruit so as to get even cooking
6. Continue turning every 5 minutes until the breadfruit is cooked
7. The breadfruit is cooked when the skin is very black and has some white ash on it
8. To break open the cooked breadfruit, simply hit it against a hard surface a couple of times
9. Use oven gloves for breaking and handling, to scoop out the flesh as the outside will be very hot
10. Serve straightaway in individual bowls with butter or maragrine spreads on it.

Boiled Cassava (Manyok Bwl)

Ingredients

- 1 kg **Cassava Root** – young to just matured
- 2 teaspoon **sugar** (optional)

Method

1. Peel the cassava, wash thoroughly and cut to desired size
2. The smaller the pieces, the faster the cooking process

3. Place in a deep pan with previously boiled water to cover it
4. Add the sugar to it. Some cassavas are naturally sweet while others can have a bland taste to it. Adding a tiny bit of sugar improves the overall taste
5. Boil until the cassava is cooked through. At least 20 to 25 minutes
6. Remove from heat and drain in a colander
7. Can be served hot but best it to allow to cool for a few minutes before serving
8. Arrange in a serving dish and serve
9. Great as an accompaniment to main dishes such as curries and stews.

Preparation time: 5 minutes
Cooking time: 25 minutes

Red Emperor Snapper Broth (Bouyon Bourzwa)

Ingredients

- 1.5 kilo of **red emperor snapper** fish
- 1 medium **onion** sliced
- 2 medium **tomatoes** cubed
- 3 medium **potatoes** peeled and cubed
- 2 cloves **garlic** grated
- 1 inch **ginger** grated
- 3 sprigs **thyme**
- 1 tablespoon **tomato puree**
- 6 tablespoon **sunflower oil**
- **salt and pepper**
- 3 **bilimbis** cut in quarters lengthways

Method

1. Clean the fish, cut it in pieces and season with salt and pepper. Heat the oil in a fry-pan on a fairly high heat and fry the fish in small batches to seal the juices in the fish. Remove from heat and set aside
2. Heat 3 tablespoon oil in a saucepan on medium heat. Fry the onions, garlic and ginger to soften. Add the fish, tomato, bilimbis, tomato puree and thyme and mix
3. Add the potatoes and warm water to cover the fish pieces. Cover and simmer for 15 to 20 minutes or until the fish has cooked through
4. Season with salt and pepper. Best served with rice and freshly ground chilli sauce.

Lentils with Bacon
(Lantiy Avek Bekonn)

Ingredients

- 2 cups of **red lentils**
- 250 grams of **bacon cubes**
- 2 tablespoon **sunflower oil**
- Teaspoon each of **thyme** and **parsley**
- **Salt** and **ground pepper**
- **Water**

Method

1. Pour 2 cups of red lentils in a bowl and wash thoroughly
2. Transfer the lentils into a medium pan, add 4 cups of water and bring to the boil on a medium to high heat, add the oil
3. Reduce heat to medium to low and cook the lentils are until soft and creamy to your liking, stirring frequently
4. Add bacon and cook for a further five minutes
5. Add water as necessary
6. Add thyme and parsley
7. Add salt and pepper to taste
8. Serve as a side dish with main course and preferably rice.

Tuna Kebabs (Broset Ton)

Ingredients

- 750 grams **yellow fin tuna**
- 2 medium **onions** cut into 1-inch squares
- 2 **green capsicums** cut into 1-inch squares
- Half a kilo **cherry tomatoes** or 2 **tomatoes** cut into 1-inch squares
- 1 tablespoon chopped **parsley**
- 4 tablespoon **sunflower or olive oil**
- 1 teaspoon **salt**
- Half teaspoon **pepper**
- 2 **garlic** cloves finely grated

55

4. Thread a piece of onion, tuna cube, tomato, tuna cube and capsicum on a skewer and repeat until the skewer is full
5. Brush each kebab with some of the excess marinade
6. Spray oil on a griddle pan and heat it until it is very hot
7. Grill the kebabs four at a time, 1 minute each side (tuna cooks fast)
8. Remove immediately when cooked, allow to rest for 2 minutes and serve immediately

- Half inch **ginger** finely grated
- Juice from a big **lime**
- 8 **skewers** (if wooden ones are used, soak in water for at least 10 minutes)

Method

1. Clean the tuna and cut into 1-inch cubes
2. Make a marinade from the oil, garlic, ginger, lime juice, salt, pepper and chopped parsley
3. Place the tuna cubes in the marinade and allow to rest in the refrigerator for at least half an hour

Bird Eggs Omelette
(Lomelet Dizef Zwazo)

Ingredients

- 6 **birds' eggs**
- half of a medium **onion** finely sliced (optional)
- tablespoon of finely cut **spring onion** (optional)
- 2 tablespoons of **sunflower oil**
- **Salt and pepper** to taste

Method

1. Crack the eggs into a mixing bowl with salt, pepper and onion. Beat well with a fork
2. Heat the oil in a medium frying pan on medium heat, and once hot add the eggs and move the pan around to spread the mixture out evenly
3. Once the omelette begins to cook, sprinkle the spring onions and stir a little
4. Using a spatula, lift the edges of the omelette, then fold it over in half
5. If preferred, the omelette can be flipped over to cook both sides well done.

Bonito Curry (Kari Bonit)

Ingredients

- 1.5 kg fresh **bonito** cut into bite size
- 1 medium **onion** diced
- 2 cloves **garlic** grated
- 1 inch **ginger** finely grated
- 3 heaped tablespoon of **dark curry powder**
- 1 teaspoon of **turmeric** powder
- Half teaspoon **cumin seed**
- 8 **curry leaves**
- 1 tablespoon of **tamarind paste** diluted in one cup of warm water

- 1 tablespoon of **tomato paste**
- 3 tablespoons of **sunflower oil**
- **Salt and pepper**
- 3 sprigs of **thyme**

Method

1. Season the bonito pieces with salt and pepper
2. In a deep pan, heat the oil and fry the onion until soft
3. Add the curry powder, turmeric powder, curry leaves and roast for 2 to 3 minutes
4. Add half of the garlic and ginger and stir

well to release the fragrance (1 to 2 minutes)

5. Add the fish pieces and stir gently so that the fish pieces are browned and sealed

6. Add the diluted tamarind juice and stir gently so as not to break up the bonito

7. Add the tomato paste and mix well

8. Reduce to low heat and if necessary add a little warm water

9. Cook for 5 minutes (bonito cooks fast)

10. Add the remainder of the garlic, ginger followed by the thyme, salt and pepper to taste and mix gently

11. Remove from the heat when the fish is cooked and a good consistency is achieved with the sauce

12. Arrange in a serving dish and serve hot.

50c
SEYCHELLES

Chicken Coconut Curry (Diguoise Style)

Ingredients

- 1.5 kgs **chicken** cut in bite sizes with bone, seasoned with **salt and pepper**
- **Onion** 1 medium – Diced
- **Garlic** 2 cloves – Finely grated
- **Ginger** – 1 inch finely grated
- 8 **curry leaves**
- 2 sprigs of **thyme** cleaned
- **Salt**
- **Pepper**
- 2 teaspoon **turmeric powder**

- 2 tablespoon **curry powder**
- 2 tablespoon **Sunflower Oil**
- Freshly squeezed **milk from 2 grated coconuts**
- Fresh **cinnamon leaves** (optional)

Method

1. In a medium size pan, either steam the chicken (preferred) or boil the chicken pieces in approx 100 ml water
2. Steam until the chicken is cooked through, set aside in a bowl
3. In another pan on medium heat 2 tablespoons of oil and fry the onions until

soft after which add the curry powder,
turmeric and curry leaves (karipile)

4.   Add the steamed chicken pieces and
     stir well
5.   Pour in the coconut milk and simmer a
     little until the coconut milk starts bubbling
6.   Add the garlic, ginger and thyme
7.   Simmer for 20 to 25 minutes
8.   When cooked, season to taste
9.   Remove from heat and if you wish to
     give some aroma to the dish, put some
     fresh cinnamon leaves cut in 2 in the
     sauce and cover until you are ready
     to serve
10. Best served with hot rice and chutneys.

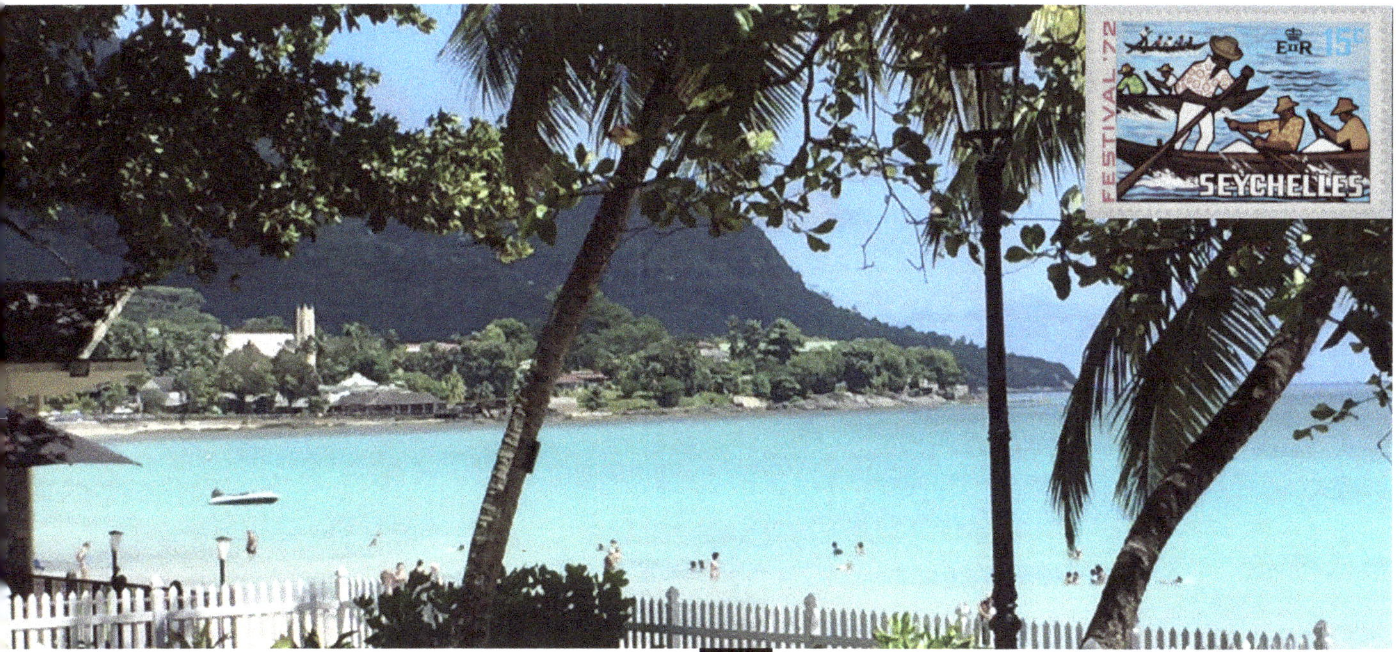
FESTIVAL '72
EIIR 15c
SEYCHELLES

ROYAL VISIT 1972
20c
SEYCHELLES

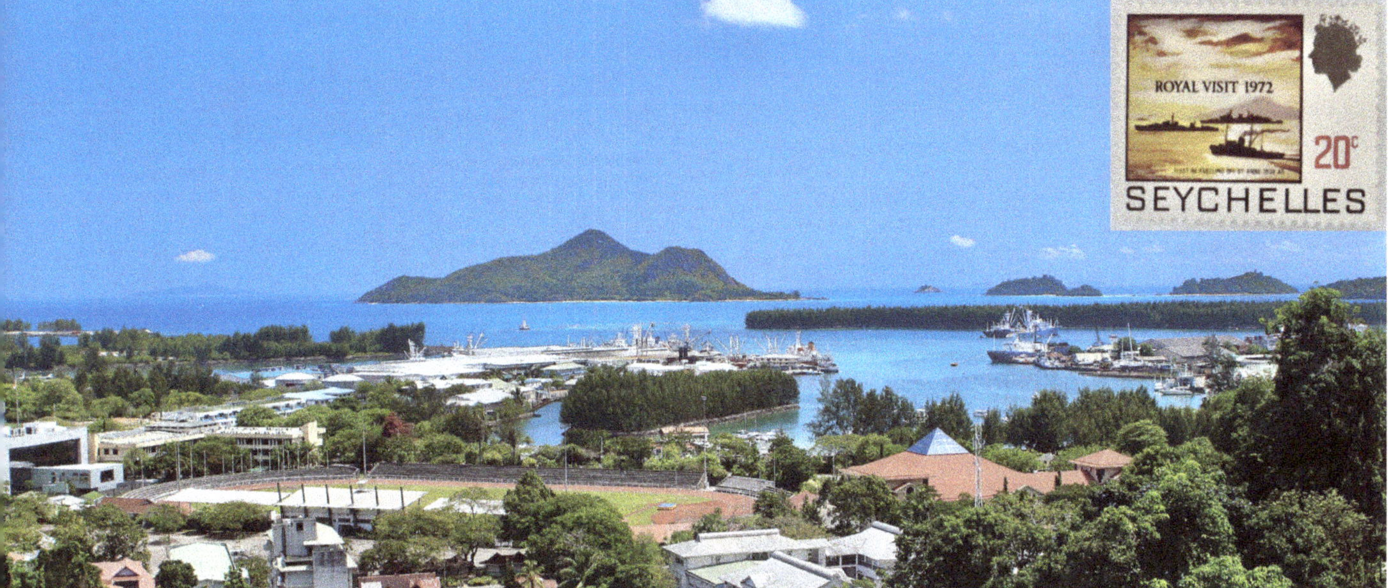

Chicken Curry Masala (Kari Poule)

Ingredients

- 1.5 kgs **chicken** cut in bite sizes with bones in, seasoned with salt and pepper
- **Onion** 1 medium – diced
- 3 medium **potatoes** peeled and cubed
- **Garlic** 2 cloves – finely grated
- 8 **curry leaves**
- 1 teaspoon **salt**
- Half teaspoon **pepper**
- 1 teaspoon **turmeric powder**
- 4 tablespoon medium to hot **curry powder**
- 2 tablespoon **sunflower oil**
- **Coriander or parsley leaves** for garnishing (optional)

Method

1. Wash and pat dry the cut up chicken properly, set aside in a mixing bowl
2. In a deep pan, heat the sunflower oil on a medium to high heat
3. Add the onion and half of the garlic and stir until the onions are softened
4. Add to the pan the curry leaves and continuing stirring to release the fragrance
5. Do not allow onions to brown
6. Add the curry powder and turmeric

powder and stir to roast for about
2 minutes
7. Add the chicken pieces and continue
stirring until the contents of the pan are
well mixed
8. Add the cubed potatoes and mix
thoroughly
9. Reduce the heat to medium to low and
partially cover the pan
10. This allows the chicken to release it own
natural juices
11. Stir every 3 to 5 minutes
12. If necessary, add water or chicken stock a
little at a time to the pan

13. After 10 to 15 minutes check to see if the
potatoes are cooked through
14. Add the remaining garlic, salt and pepper,
stir well and remove from the heat
immediately
15. Season to taste
16. Transfer to serving dish. Coriander or
parsley leaves may be used as garnishing
17. Best served hot with white rice and choice
of chutneys.

71

Chicken Stew (Stew Poul)

Ingredients

- 1.5 kg fresh **chicken** cut into bite size bones included
- 1 medium **onion** diced
- 3 cloves **garlic** grated
- 1 inch **ginger** finely grated
- 3 medium very ripe fresh **tomatoes** chopped
- 5 medium **potatoes**, peeled, cut into quarters lengthwise and patted dry
- 2 tablespoon **tomato paste**
- 1 teaspoon chopped **parsley**
- 1 tablespoon of **tomato paste**
- 500 ml **sunflower oil** for frying
- **Salt and pepper**
- 3 sprigs of **thyme**

Method

1. Pat the chicken dry and season with salt and pepper
2. Heat the 500ml of oil in a deep fry pan and fry the chicken until lightly brown Remove from pan and set aside
3. Fry the cut potatoes in the same oil until lightly brown and not totally cooked, set aside

4.   In a deep saucepan, heat 3 tablespoons sunflower oil and brown the onion
5.   Add half the garlic, ginger to the pan and stir for a minute to release the fragrance
6.   Add the chopped tomatoes and tomato paste, half of the thyme and parsley and stir well
7.   Allow the mixture to simmer for about 5 minutes, adding some warm water if necessary
8.   When the sauce has reached a nice consistency, add the chicken pieces and potatoes and stir gently
9.   Allow to cook for about 10 minutes on low heat, adding water a little at a time Chicken stock can be substituted to give added flavour
10.   At the end of the 10 minutes, add the rest of the garlic, ginger, parsley and thyme, salt and pepper and stir gently
11.   Remove from heat and transfer to a serving dish immediately. Best served hot with rice and chutneys.

Seychelles Facts & Figures

Geography: Indian Ocean, **Latitude:** 4.6796° S, **Longitude:** 55.4920°E, **Time Zone:** Greenwich Meridian Time (GMT) + 4 hours, 115 islands scattered over 1,374,000 km2 of ocean.

Principal inhabited islands are **Mahe, Praslin** and **La Digue. Victoria,** the capital is on the main island, **Mahe.** Tropical climate with temperature ranging from 24C to 33C.

Population: 96,800 at the end of December 2018. (National Bureau of Statistics. **Languages:** English, French and Creole - the local dialect. **Religion:** Predominantly of christian faith. **Currency:** Rupees and Cents. 1 rupee = 100 cents. **Primary Industries:** Tourism, Fishing and Financial Services.
Electricity: 220.240 volts AC 50 Hz. **Water:** Treated and is safe for drinking. **Business Hours:** Monday to Friday. 0800 to 1600 hours.

Lyrics of the Seychelles National Anthem - Koste Seselwa

Sesel ou menm nou sel patri	**Seychelles, our only motherland**
Kot nou viv dan larmoni	**Where we live in harmony**
Lazwa, lanmour ek lape	**Happiness, love and peace**
Nou remersye Bondye	**We give thanks to God**
Preserv labote nou pei	**Preserve the beauty of our country**
Larises nou losean	**The riches of our oceans**
En leritaz byen presye	**A precious heritage**
Pour boner nou zanfan	**For the happiness of our children**
Reste touzour dan linite	**Live forever in unity**
Fer monte nou paviyon	**Raise our flag**
Ansanm pou tou leternite	**Together for all eternity**
Koste Seselwa!	**Join together all Seychellois**

Corned Beef Sauted (Bouli Beef)

Ingredients

- 1 tin **corned beef** 425 grams
- Half tin **baby peas** 250 grams
- 1 medium **onion** sliced
- Half teaspoon **cumin seeds**
- 3 chopped **chillies** (optional)
- 2 tablespoon **sunflower oil**
- **Salt and pepper**

Method

1. Remove the corned beef from the tin and mash it up
2. Open the tin of peas, drain and set aside
3. In a deep fry pan, heat the oil and soften the onion together with the cumin seeds until the latter crackle
4. Add the corned beef to the fry pan and mix well
5. Add the baby peas and continue stirring until well mixed
6. Add the chillies, a little salt (corned beef is already salty) and pepper
7. Mix well and remove from heat immediately
8. Transfer to serving dish and serve hot.

Crab Curry Masala (Kari Krab)

Ingredients

- 1.5 kgs cleaned and uncooked **krab giraffe or mud crab** cut in bite sizes and claws cracked to permit curry sauce to penetrate the shell
- **Onion** 1 medium – diced
- 3 medium ripe **tomatoes** diced
- **Garlic** 2 cloves – finely grated
- 1 inch **ginger** finely grated
- 8 **curry leaves**
- 1 teaspoon **salt**
- Half teaspoon **pepper**
- 1 teaspoon **turmeric powder**
- 4 tablespoon medium to hot **curry powder**
- 2 tablespoon **sunflower oil**
- **Coriander or parsley leaves** for garnishing (optional)

Method

1. In a deep pan, heat the sunflower oil on a medium to high heat
2. Add the onion and half of the garlic and ginger and stir until the onions are softened
3. Add to the pan the curry leaves and continuing stirring to release the fragrance. Do not allow onions to brown
4. Add the curry powder and turmeric powder and stir to roast for about 2 minutes

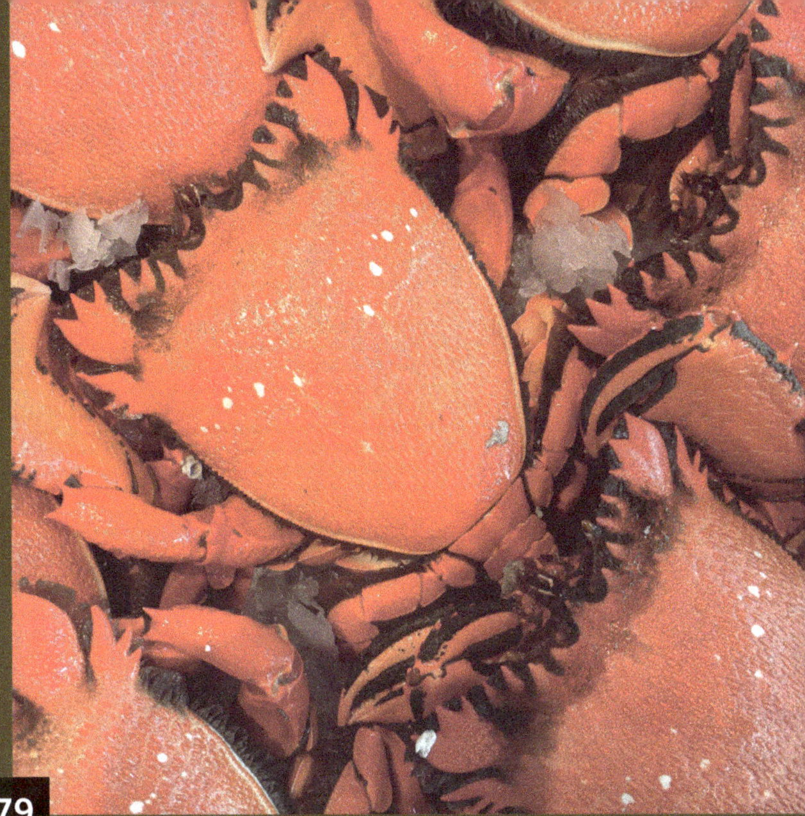

5. Add the diced tomatoes and mix until you get a thick paste
6. Add warm water and bring to the boil
7. Add the crab pieces and mix thoroughly
8. Add more more warm water until all crab pieces are just covered
9. Reduce heat and simmer for 10 to 15 minutes or until the sauce has thickened
10. Stir every 3 to 5 minutes. Cinnamon leaves may be added to give to fragrant taste to the dish
11. Add the remaining garlic, ginger salt and pepper, stir well and remove from the heat immediately
12. Season to taste. Transfer to serving dish
13. Best served hot with white rice and choice of chutneys.

Creole Pulao (Plo kreole)

Ingredients

- 1.5 kg **chicken** cut in pieces, skin removed, bone in
- 0.5 kgs **salted sausages** (may be omitted for non pork eaters)
- 0.5 kgs **salted pork** (may be omitted for non pork eaters)
- 5 cups of **long grain rice** (Basmati rice preferred)
- 1 **Onion** sliced
- 3 cloves **garlic** minced
- 1 inch **ginger** grated
- 8 **cloves** whole
- 8 **cloves** ground

- 3 teaspoons **turmeric powder**
- leaves from 5 sprigs **thyme**
- 1 tablespoon of chopped **parsely**
- 3 tablespoon **oil**
- 1 tablespoon **salt**
- 1 teaspoon **pepper**
- 10 **curry leaves**

Method

1. Drain and set aside. When cool, cut sausages and pork into bite sizes
2. In a deep saucepan, heat 3 tablespoons oil
3. Add onions and curry leaves to the pan and allow to soften
4. Add the garlic, ginger, ground cloves and stir well
5. Add the turmeric and roast with the other ingredients

6. Add the chicken and keep stirring until the chicken has sealed well
7. The sausage and pork, thyme, and whole cloves can then be added and mixed well.
8. Season with salt and pepper
9. Reduce the heat to medium to low heat to allow all the flavours to blend and for the meat to release some natural juices for about 10 minutes
10. In the meantime, in another deep saucepan with a heavy base, bring the washed rice in an equal amount of water plus 1 cup just to the stage where the rice starts showing a translucent colour without being cooked and remove from the heat immediately
11. Spoon the seasoned meat mixture into the rice and stir well
12. Cook on a medium heat with the lid on and well sealed
13. After 5 minutes remove the lid of the pan and give the mixture a stir to ensure the meat and rice is well distributed, and level the mixture and cover and seal the pan once more and reduce heat to a low heat and cook for a further 10 minutes
14. After the 10 minutes are up, remove the pan from the heat and allow to stand for at least 15 minutes for the cooking process to continue with the lid still on
15. Serve while still hot with chutneys and salads.

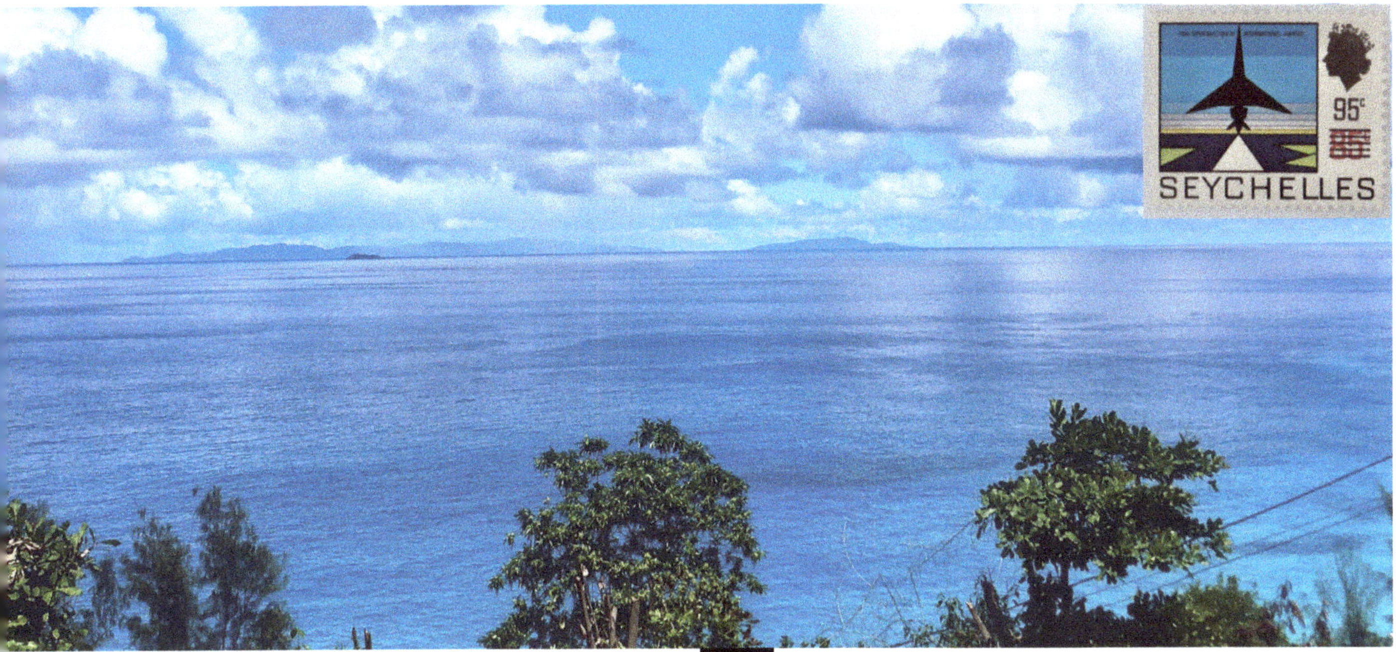

95c
SEYCHELLES

FISHERMAN
UNIVERSAL
ADULT
SUFFRAGE
1967
15
CENTS
SEYCHELLES

83

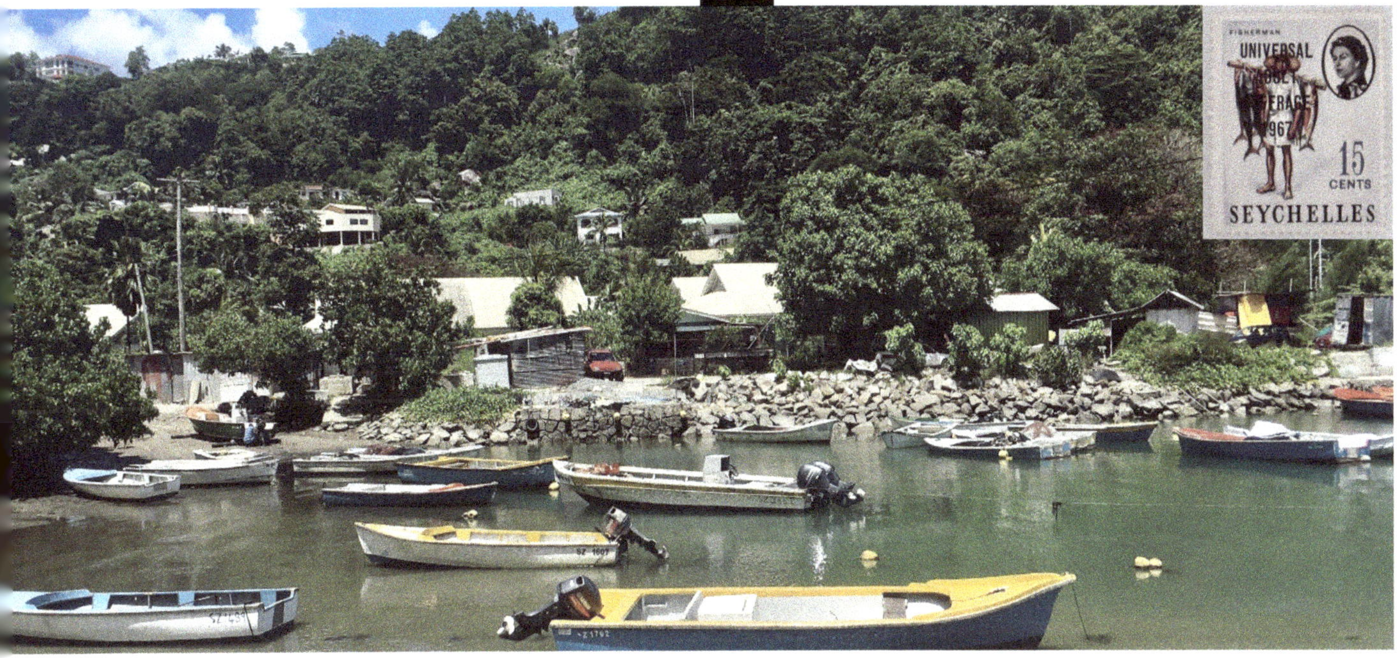

Fish Curry with Tamarind
(Kari Pwason Tanmarin)

Ingredients

- 1.5 kgs **fish** of any type (white meat preferred) cut in bite sizes
- **Onion** 1 medium – Diced
- **Garlic** 2 cloves – Finely grated
- **Ginger** – 1 inch finely grated
- 1 tablespoon of **tamarind paste** diluted in one cup of warm water
- 8 **curry leaves**
- 1 teaspoon **turmeric powder**
- 3 heaped tablespoon **dark curry powder**
- 4 tablespoon **sunflower oil**

Method

1. Season the fish with salt and pepper
2. In a pan on medium, heat the oil and fry the onions, garlic, ginger together with the curry powder, turmeric and curry leaves
3. Add the fish pieces and stir gently so that the fish pieces are browned on all sides and sealed
4. Add the tamarind paste. Allow to cook on low heat
5. Add more water if required
6. Season to taste with salt and pepper
7. Remove from heat when fish is cooked and a good consistency is achieved in the sauce
8. Best served immediately with hot rice and chutneys. Can be garnished with coriander leaves.

Fried Fish – Rabbit Fish/Trevally/Mackerel (Kordonnyen/Karang/Makro)

Ingredients

- Any **fish** of your choice from the 3 most popular ones above
- **Salt and Pepper**
- **Oil**

Method

1. Scale and gut your fish
2. For all the above fishes, make sure you scrape the skin well until a dark slick is not seen when you keep scraping them
3. Rabbit fish and mackerels are best fried whole. Make 4 or 5 slits diagonally on each side. Trevally should be cut up in pieces in size of your preference
4. Pat the fish dry. This minimises spluttering of oil when frying
5. Make a rubbing mixture with salt and pepper
6. Rub this mixture liberally in the slits of the fish or fish pieces
7. Heat the oil on a medium heat in a large fry-pan which can accommodate whole fishes or many pieces of fish at a time
8. Allow the oil to reach the correct temperature before frying starts and also do not fry on high heat otherwise the fish will turn dark brown before it is cooked inside
9. Allow the fish to fry gently to your preferred style, turning only once
10. Trevally is best enjoyed when still a little moist but Seychellois prefer their rabbit fish and mackerel more dried
11. Remove from fry pan when done and transfer to a dish lined with absorbent kitchen paper to drain excess oil before serving
12. Serve on its own or with white rice and spinach broth.

Goat Curry (Kari Kabri)

Ingredients

- 750 grams of **goat meat** bone in
- **Onion** 1 medium – Diced
- **Garlic** 2 cloves – Finely grated
- **Ginger** – 1 inch finely grated
- 1 tablespoon of **tamarind paste** diluted in one cup of warm water
- 8 **curry leaves**
- 1 teaspoon **turmeric powder**
- 3 heaped tablespoon **dark curry powder**
- 4 tablespoon **sunflower oil**
- 1 teaspoon chopped **parsley**
- 1 teaspoon **thyme**
- 4 tablespoons of **brown vinegar**
- 3 **scotch bonnet chilli** (piman kabri) quartered
- **Salt**
- **Pepper**

Method

1. Clean and cut the meat into cubes, remove any sinews but keep the bones
2. Place the washed meat in a mixing bowl with the 4 tablespoons of brown vinegar and allow to soak for 15 minutes

This process tames the wild smell and taste of the goat meat

3. After the 15 minutes are up, drain, wash and pat the meat dry
4. In a deep pan, heat the oil on a medium to high heat
5. Add the onions and half of the garlic and ginger and stir until the onions are soft
6. Add the curry leaves and continue stirring to release the fragrance
7. Add the curry powder and stir for 2 minutes to roast
8. Add the meat and continue stirring until all the contents of the pan are thoroughly mixed

9. Reduce heat to medium and add a little water if necessary and cook with lid on for 5 minutes
10. After 5 minutes, stir to mix the contents of the pan and reduce to low heat
11. Cook for a further 25 to 30 minutes with lid on until the meat is tender, adding water as needed
12. Once the meat is tender, add the garlic, thyme, parsley, salt and pepper, and chillies and stir to mix well
13. Cook for a further 5 minutes uncovered
14. Arrange in a serving dish and serve immediately.

SEYCHELLES
POSTAGE
REVENUE
6c

SEYCHELLES
5c

Grilled Mackerel (Makro Grlye)

Ingredients

- 6 fresh **Indian mackerel** gutted, gilled, scaled and cleaned with skin on
- 1 medium **onion** diced
- 1 inch **ginger** grated
- 3 to 4 cloves **garlic** finely crushed
- 4 **bilimbi** crushed – may be omitted and replaced with tomato if this is not available
- Crushed fresh **chillis** (to your taste) – kreoles like their grilled fish with plenty of chilli (hot)
- 1 teaspoon **turmeric**
- 1 medium **tomato** finely diced (optional)
- 4 tablespoon of **oil**
- **Salt and pepper** to taste
- 3 sprigs of **thyme** chopped up
- **Parsley** to garnish
- Fresh **'bigarade' (quamqat)** to squeeze on the grilled fish

Method

1. Make 3 to 4 slits on each side of the cleaned fish
2. Mix all the all ingredients together in a bowl
3. Using a spoon, carefully put the mixed ingredients generously in each slit in the fish and if any is left over, insert inside the fish as well. Allow to marinate for at least 15 minutes, preferably in the fridge as

mackerel gets soft easily in warm
temperatures.

**Barbeque grilling method: This is the preferred
method of Seychellois.**

1. Prepare your barbeque (charcoal preferred)
    until the coal is only glowing, without the
    flames. Oil your grill and on it place pieces
    of stem of coconut leaves at 2 inches
    interval to take the entire length of the fish.
    This is to prevent the fish from sticking to
    the grill and to keep the skin intact. A bbq
    meat holder is also handy for cooking and
    also helps turning the fish
2. Allow to cook for 10 minutes on each side.
    Ensure that you have water handy to douse
    any flame as your marinate contains oil
    which can encourage the flaming.

If using a kettle barbeque, it is a good idea to
keep the lid covered for the first 5 minutes to
speed up the cooking process and to keep the
fish moist.

Remember there is no hard and fast rule or
any for how long it takes for the fish to cook.
The above cooking times are guides only. The
cooking length all depends on the cooking
temperature. Like with any fish, the simple trick
is not to allow the fish to cook until it is dry
and hard.

Main Ingredients used in Seychelles Creole Cuisine

Grilled Red Emperor Snapper
(Bourzwa Griye)

Ingredients

- 1.3 kgs whole **Bourzwa** gutted, gilled, scaled and cleaned with skin on
- 1 medium **onion** diced
- 1 inch **ginger** grated
- 3 to 4 cloves **garlic** finely crushed
- 4 **bilimbi** crushed – may be omitted and replaced with tomato if this is not available.
- Crushed fresh **chillis** (to your taste) – kreoles like their grilled fish with plenty of chilli (hot)

- 1 teaspoon **turmeric**
- 1 medium **tomato** finely diced
- 4 tablespoon of **oil**
- **Salt and pepper** to taste
- 3 sprigs of **thyme** chopped up
- **Parsley** to garnish
- Fresh **lime** to squeeze on the grilled fish

Method

1. Make at least 4 to 5 slits on each side of the cleaned fish, with each slit about an inch apart
2. Mix all the all ingredients together in a bowl
3. Using a spoon, carefully put the mixed ingredients generously in each slit in the

fish and if any is left over, insert inside the fish as well. Allow to marinate for at least 15 minutes.

Oven method:

1. Pre-heat the oven to 180 degrees celsius
2. Place the marinated fish in an ovenproof dish, big enough to hold the whole fish and place in the centre of the oven and cook uncovered for 35 to 40 minutes
3. After 20 minutes, open the oven, and baste the fish in its own juice and allow to cook for the rest of the rest of the time
4. After the 40 minutes are up, using a sharp knife, pierce in the thickest part of the fish
5. If the knife slides in, without any resistance, the fish is cooked through. Turn the oven to grilling mode and allow the skin to be grilled until see it start to turn a little brown. This should take no more than 5 minutes
6. Remove the fish, garnish with the parsely, squeeze the lime on it and serve immediately.

Barbeque grilling method:
This is the preferred method of Seychellois.

1. Prepare your barbeque (charcoal preferred) until the coal is only glowing, without the flames. Place pieces of stem of palm fronds on the grill at 2 inches interval to take the length of the fish
2. This is to prevent the fish from sticking to the grill and to keep the skin intact. Allow to cook for 15 minutes on each side.

Have water handy to douse any flame
3. If using a kettle barbeque, it is a good idea to keep the lid covered for the first 10 minutes to speed up the cooking process and to keep the fish moist. Again, use the knife test above to check that the fish is cooked through
4. Remember there is no hard and fast rule or any for how long it takes for the fish to cook. Cooking times are for guide only and will depend on the temperature of the fire and the fat content of the fish. Like with any fish, the simple trick is not to allow the fish to cook until it is dry and hard
5. Serve with rice, chutneys or fresh green salad.

"Seychelles National Flower - The Tropicbird Orchid."

Limpets Coconut Curry
(Kari Koko Bernik)

Ingredients

- 1 kg cleaned **limpets** and shells discarded
- **Onion** 1 medium – Diced
- **Garlic** 2 cloves – Finely grated
- **Ginger** – 1 inch finely grated
- 8 **curry leaves**
- 21teaspoon **turmeric powder**
- 2 tablespoon **curry powder**
- 2 tablespoon **Sunflower Oil**
- Freshly squeezed **milk from 2 grated coconuts**
- Salt and pepper

101

Method

1. Wash the limpets and make sure all small pieces of shell are removed
2. In a medium pan, boil some water with salt added. Add the limpet to the pan and boil for 3 to 5 minutes. Drain and set aside
3. Heat the oil in another saucepan on medium heat. Fry the onions lightly until soft and add the curry power, turmeric and curry leaves and stir well. Add the boiled limpets and mix well
4. Add the coconut milk and lower the heat
5. Once the coconut milk stars bubbling, add garlic, ginger and cinnamon leaves and stir
6. Simmer on low heat for 10 minutes
7. When cooked, adjust seasoning
8. Best served with hot rice and chutneys.

Lobster Curry (Kari Oumar) with Pumpkin Leaves

Ingredients

- 1.5 kgs cleaned and uncooked **lobster** cut in bite sizes and legs cracked to permit curry sauce to penetrate the shell
- 1 medium **onion** – diced
- 2 cloves **garlic** – finely grated
- 1 inch **ginger** finely grated
- 8 **curry leaves**
- 1 teaspoon **salt**
- Half teaspoon **pepper**
- 1 teaspoon **turmeric powder**
- 4 tablespoon medium to hot **curry powder**
- 2 tablespoon **sunflower oil**
- 1 bunch of washed **young pumpkin leaves**

Method

1. In a deep pan, heat the sunflower oil on a medium to high heat
2. Add the onion and half of the garlic and ginger and stir until the onions are softened
3. Add to the pan the curry leaves and continuing stirring to release the fragrance
4. Do not allow onions to brown
5. Add the curry powder and turmeric powder and stir to roast for about 2 minutes

6. Add one cup warm water and bring to the boil
7. Reduce heat and add lobster pieces and mix thoroughly
8. Add more water until the lobster pieces are just covered
9. Reduce heat and simmer for 5 minutes – lobsters cook very fast
10. Add the pumpkin leaves and stalk, followed by the rest of the garlic and ginger and mix
11. Add salt and pepper, stir well and cover for 5 minutes to allow the pumpkin leaves to just wilt
12. Remove from the heat and season to taste
13. Transfer to serving dish and serve with hot white rice.

Octopus Coconut Curry
(Kari Koko Zourit)

Ingredients

- 1 medium size **octopus** (approx 1 kg)
- **Onion** 1 medium – diced
- **Garlic** 2 cloves – finely grated
- **Ginger** – 2 cms finely grated
- 8 **curry leaves**
- **Salt**
- **Pepper**
- 2 tsp **turmeric powder**
- 2 tablespoon **sunflower oil**
- Freshly squeezed **milk from 2 grated coconuts**
- 6 Fresh **cinnamon leaves** cut in two

Method

1. In a large pan, boil the octopus until tender (adding vinegar or green papaya to the saucepan speeds up the tenderizing process)
2. Drain and cool in cold water and clean properly. We recommend removing the suckers on the tentacles
3. Cut the tentacles in small rings of about 1 cm in size. Cut the body into bite size pieces
4. Heat the oil in another saucepan on medium heat
5. Fry the onion lightly, avoid browning it
6. Add the curry leaves and turmeric to the pan and give a quick stir
7. Add the octopus and mix well
8. Add the coconut milk
9. Once the coconut milk starts bubbling, add the garlic, ginger and cinnamon leaves and stir
10. Add salt and pepper
11. Simmer for 10 to 15 minutes
12. When cooked, adjust seasoning.

Octopus Salad

Ingredients

- 1 kg **octopus**
- 1 medium **brown onion** sliced
- 2 tbsps **sunflower oil**
- 10ml **vinegar**
- Pinch of **salt**
- **Pepper** to liking
- 1 tsp of **sugar** (optional)
- 1 diced medium **tomato**
- 1 small diced **red capsicum**
- 1 small diced **yellow capsicum**
- 1 small diced **green capsicum**

Method

1. Boil the octopus until tender, at least one hour Allow to cool and clean thoroughly, removin the skin and tentacles
2. Cut into 1 cm pieces and set aside
3. Soak the sliced onions in salted warm water for 10 minutes
4. Squeeze the onions to remove all the water and place in a bowl
5. Make a dressing with the vinegar, salt and pepper and mix with the onion
6. Place the octopus in a serving bowl together with the tomato and capsicums and pour the dressing over it
7. Garnish with spring onions.

Okra Curry (Kari Lalo)

Ingredients

- 500 grams **okra**, washed, top and tail removed and cut in 1 cm slices across
- 1 medium **onion** – diced
- 1 medium **tomato** diced
- 8 **curry leaves**
- 2 cloves **garlic** – finely grated
- 1 inch **ginger** finely grated
- 1 teaspoon **salt**
- Half teaspoon **pepper**
- Half teaspoon **cumin seeds**
- Half teaspoon **mustard seeds**
- 2 tablespoons **mild powder**
- 2 tablespoons **sunflower oil**

Method

1. Heat the sunflower oil on a medium heat
2. Add the mustard and cummin seeds
3. When the seeds start popping, add the onions and curry leaves
4. Sir until onion softens
5. Add the garlic and ginger and continue stirring and do not allow the ingredients to go brown
6. Add the curry power and stir
7. Toss in the okra pieces and keep stirring until all mixed
8. Add the diced tomatoes and stir well
9. Reduce to low heat and cooked covered for a few minutes
10. Add salt and pepper to taste and add a little water if required
11. The okra should still have some crunch to it
12. Remove from heat and transfer to serving dish and serve with hot white rice.

Poached Spicy Trevally
(Letoufe Pwason)

Ingredients

- 1 kilo of **trevally** cubed or sliced in cutlets if small trevally is used
- 1 medium **onion** sliced
- 1 medium **tomato** cubed
- 2 cloves **garlic** grated
- half inch **ginger** grated
- 4 sprigs **thyme**
- 3 tablespoon **sunflower oil**
- Half teaspoon **salt** and pinch of **ground black pepper**
- 6 **bilimbis** cut in quarters lengthways
- 2 crushed **chillies** (optional)

Method

1. Clean the fish properly and cut it in pieces
2. Season with salt and pepper and set aside
3. Heat the oil in a saucepan on medium setting
4. Fry the onions lightly add the tomatoes and half of the ginger and garlic and stir well until onion is soft
5. Add the fish pieces and stir gently and reduce the heat
6. Add enough warm water to cover the fish pieces and cover the pan
7. After 5 minutes, add the bilimbis, thyme and the rest of the garlic and ginger, salt and pepper
8. Using a wooden spoon gently mix the contents of the pan from side to side
9. Cook covered on a gentle heat for a further 5 minutes. Do not allow to dry out
10. Remove from the heat and adjust seasoning
11. Chillies can be added at this stage if desired.
12. Transfer to a serving dish and serve while still hot with rice.

113

Pork Curry (Kari Pork)

Ingredients

- 1.5 kgs **pork** cut in bite sizes. Discard as much fat as possible. Some skin can be left Lean pork makes for a healthier choice
- **Onion** 1 medium – diced
- **Garlic** 2 cloves – finely grated
- 8 **curry leaves**
- 1 teaspoon **salt**
- Half teaspoon **pepper**
- 1 teaspoon **turmeric powder**
- 4 tablespoon medium to hot **curry powder**
- 2 tablespoon **sunflower oil**

Method

1. Wash, and parboil the pork, drain and pat dry the cut up pork properly, set aside in a mixing bowl
2. In a deep pan, heat the sunflower oil on a medium to high heat
3. Add the onion and half of the garlic and stir until the onions are softened
4. Add to the pan the curry leaves and continuing stirring to release the fragrance
5. Do not allow onions to brown
6. Add the curry powder and turmeric powder and stir to roast for about 2 minutes
7. Add the pork pieces and continue stirring until the contents of the pan are well mixed
8. Reduce the heat to medium to low and partially cover the pan
9. Add some water because pork is generally a dry meat
10. Stir every 3 to 5 minutes
11. If necessary, add water, a little at a time to the pan
12. Pork does not take long to cook and should be ready in 15 minutes
13. Add the remaining garlic, salt and pepper, stir well and remove from the heat immediately
14. Season to taste
15. Transfer to serving dish. Parsley leaves may be used as garnishing
16. Best served hot with white rice and choice of chutneys.

Pot Roasted Pork
(Pork Roti dan Marmit)

Ingredients

- 1.5 kgs **pork shoulder or leg** tied
- 3 medium size **onions,** peeled and
  cut in quarters
- 1 bunch of **thyme**
- 10 cloves of **garlic** peeled and
  roughly smashed
- 4 tablespoon **sunflower oil** to just cover
  the bottom of the pan entirely
- 20 ml warm **water**
- **Salt and pepper**

Method

1. Wash the pork properly removing any
   excess bits. Pat dry and season with salt,
   pepper and half of the thyme
2. Heat the oil in a deep pan on high heat
   and place the pork in the pan, rind side down
3. After a few minutes, move the pork to
   ensure the entire rind is caramelized
4. Turn the pork and caramelize the other
   sides. Reduce the heat to medium
5. Remove the pork from the pan briefly and
   add the onions, garlic and thyme. Place
   the pork back in with rind facing up
6. Add some warm water, cover the pot and
   continue cooking for at least 40 minutes
   Check every five minutes
7. Add warm water a little at a time if
   required during the cooking process to
   prevent the pan from drying out and
   burning the bottom. Test to see if the pork
   is cooked by inserting a skewer or a sharp
   knife in the thickest part. (A meat
   thermometer can be used. Optimum
   temperature 71C medium to 77C
   well done)
8. If the juice runs clear, remove from the
   heat immediately. Allow to rest for minutes
9. Add some warm water to the pan to create
   a nice gravy. Cut the pork into slices and
   arrange in a serving dish. Pour the gravy
   over the slice pork and serve immediately
   with boiled sweet potatoes or root crop of
   choice and vegetables.

Salted Fish Coconut Curry with Moringa Leaves (Kari Koko Pwason Sale ek Bred Mouroum)

Ingredients

- 1 kilo **salted fish** of any type (best; rabbit fish, grouper, dorado)
- 1 big bunch of **moringa leaves**
- 1 medium **onion** sliced
- 2 tablespoons **sunflower oil**
- 3 tablespoon **curry powder**
- 1 teaspoon **turmeric**
- 3 cloves **garlic** finely grated
- 2cm **ginger** grated
- Milk from 2 freshly grated **coconuts**
- 8 **curry leaves**
- Half teaspoon **salt**
- Pinch of **black pepper**
- 2 **cinnamon leaves** (optional)

Method

1. Clean the salted fish, discarding as much as possible of inedible parts
2. Place the fish in boiling water and cook for at least 10 minutes
3. Drain and cool under the running water
4. Remove any bones, fins, skin, leaving only the edible parts cut into bite sizes
5. In a deep frypan, heat the oil on medium heat
6. Add the onions until softened, followed by the curry powder, turmeric powder and curry leaves
7. Stir well and add the slated fish and continue stirring
8. Add the coconut milk and allow to simmer for 3 to 5 minutes until oil starts appearing
9. Add the moringa leaves, garlic and ginger
10. Add the salt and pepper and allow to simmer for at least 10 minutes on low heat
11. Add cinnamon leaves 3 minutes before removing from heat and adjust for seasoning
12. When moringa leaves are cooked remove from the heat
13. Transfer to serving dish and serve while still hot.

Salted Fish Salad
(Salad Pwason Sale)

Ingredients

- 1 kg **salted fish** of your choice. Preference of Seychellois is rabbit fish (Kordonnyen) or any white meat salted fish
- 1 **red or white onion** finely sliced
- 1 ripe but firm **tomato** roughly chopped
- 1 **sem-ripe tomato** roughly chop
- **Sunflower oil** for frying
- Dressing made up of 3 tablespoon **sunflower oil,** 2 tablespoon diluted **brown vinegar, salt, pepper** and chopped **parsley**

Method

1. In a pan of boilling water, add the fish and boil for 15 minutes to remove the salt from the fish
2. Clean the fish and discard all fins, tails and bones. Drain and allow to cool
3. In a shallow fry-pan, heat up the sunflower oil to cover the bottom of the pan until hot
4. Shallow fry the fish pieces lightly in batches and remove and drain on grease absorbent kitchen paper
5. Arrange the fish pieces in a serving dish
6. Mix the onions, tomatoes and dressing in a separate bowl
7. Pour salad dressing mix over the fish
8. Serve with hot white rice and chutneys.

121

Salted Fish Stew
(Rougay Pwason Sale)

Ingredients

- 1 kg **Salted fish** of your choice.
- 1 medium size chopped **onion**
- 3 medium ripe fresh **tomatoes** chopped
- 3 tablespoon **sunflower oil**
- 20 gm **garlic** minced
- 10 gm **ginger** grated
- 2 tablespoon **tomato concentrate**
- 3 **thyme sprigs**
- 1 tablespoon of chopped **parsely**
- **salt and pepper**

Method

1. In a pan of boiling water, add the fish and boil for 15 minutes to remove the salt from the fish. Clean the fish and discard all fins, tails and bones
2. In another saucepan, heat oil on a medium heat, sauté the onions and fresh tomatoes
3. Add garlic, ginger and stir until fragant
4. Add the tomato puree and stir well
5. Add the fish pieces and keep stirring
6. Add enough warm water to cover the mixture. Simmer on low heat for 10 minutes
7. Add thyme, parsely, salted and pepper and cook for another 5 minutes, on low heat until the sauce has achieved a good consistency
8. Garnish with parsley and serve with rice.

Salted Sausage Stew
(Rougay Pwason Sale)

Ingredients

- 8 **salted sausages**
- 1 medium size chopped **onion**
- 3 medium ripe fresh **tomatoes** chopped
- 3 tablespoon **sunflower oil**
- 20 gm **garlic** minced
- 10 gm **ginger** grated
- 2 tablespoon **tomato concentrate**
- 3 **thyme sprigs**
- 1 tablespoon of chopped **parsely**
- **salt and pepper**

Method

1. In a saucepan bring 1 litre of water to the boil and add the sausage and cook for at least 10 minutes. This process removes the salt and excess fat
2. Drain and cool and cut into one centimetre pieces, set aside
3. In another saucepan, heat oil on a medium heat, sauté the onions and fresh tomatoes
4. Add garlic, ginger and stir until fragant
5. Add the tomato puree and stir well in the mixture
6. Add the sausages and keep stirring
7. Add some water
8. Simmer on low heat for 10 minutes
9. Add thyme, parsely, salted and pepper and cook for another 5 minutes, again on low heat until the sauce has achieved a good consistency
10. Garnish with parsely
11. Can be served immediately with rice.

Spinach Broth with Fried Fish (Bouyon Bred ek Pwason Friye)

Chinese cabbage (Soupsin) or Moringa Mouroum and any fried fish.

Ingredients

- Big bunch of **any the above**
- **Fried fish.** Trevally (Karang balo is best)
- 1 medium size **brown onion**, peeled and sliced
- 2 cloves **garlic** minced
- ½ garlic grated
- 1 tablespoon **sunflower oil**
- **salt and ground pepper**
- warm water

Method

1. Wash and cut your spinach (bred)
2. Season fish pieces with salt and pepper and deep fry until golden brown, set aside
3. Heat the oil in saucepan, and soften the onions and add the spinach
4. Add the ginger and garlic and mix well
5. Add warm water, enough to just cover the spinach
6. Add the fried fish
7. Season with salt and paper
8. Reduce heat to simmer for 10 minutes
9. Remove when the spinach has just cooked through
10. Allow to stand for 5 minutes before serving.

"Landing page of the App Seychelles Creole Cuisine - available on the App Store and Google Play."

Trevally Fish Roe Salad
(Salad Dizef Karang)

Ingredients

- 2 to 3 good size fresh **trevally fish roe**
- 1 big **onion** sliced
- Dressing made from 3 tbsp of **sunflower oil**, 2 tablespoons of **brown vinegar, salt** and **ground black pepper**
- 500 ml **sunflower oil** for frying

Method

1. Wash the fish roe and boil in a saucepan for 10 minutes
2. Once cooked, rinse in cold water and allow to cool down. Cut into half inch slices lengthwise and pat dry
3. Bring oil to medium heat
4. Cook the roe slices in batches until golden brown
5. Remove and place on absorbent paper towel to soak excess oil
6. Arrange in a serving dish
7. Mix the onions with the dressing and spread over the fried fish roe
8. Serve as a side dish with main meal.

Tuna Curry in Coconut Milk (Kari Koko Ton)

Ingredients

- 1.5 kgs **tuna loin** cut in bite sizes
- **Onion** 1 medium – Diced
- **Garlic** 2 cloves – Finely grated
- **Ginger** – 1 inch finely grated
- 8 **curry leaves**
- 2 sprigs of **thyme** cleaned
- **Salt**
- **Pepper**
- 2 teaspoon **turmeric powder**
- 2 tablespoon **curry powder**
- 4 tablespoon **sunflower oil**
- Freshly squeezed **milk from 2 grated coconuts**
- Fresh **cinnamon leaves** (optional)

Method

1. Season the tuna with salt and pepper
2. Heat 2 tablespoon oil in a large fry-pan until quite hot and toss the tuna pieces in there to seal them
3. Remove from pan, the moment they lose the pink colour. Set aside in a bowl
4. In another pan on medium, heat 2 tablespoon of oil and fry the onions together with the curry powder, turmeric and curry leaves
5. Pour in the coconut milk and simmer a little until the coconut milk starts bubbling
6. Add the tuna pieces and stir well
7. Add the garlic, ginger and thyme
8. Simmer for 10 minutes on low heat
9. When cooked, season to taste
10. Remove from heat and if you wish to give some aroma to the dish, put some fresh cinnamon leaves cut in 2 in the sauce and cover until you are ready to serve
11. Best served with hot rice and chutneys.

Banana Chips

Ingredients

- 2 **green bananas**, preferably plantain
- 500 ml **sunflower oil**
- 1 teaspon **fine salt**
-

Great as a sundowner snack.

Method

1. Peel the green skin off the bananas, wash and pat dry
2. Cut the bananas in fine rings or slice over a mandolin lengthwise
3. Heat the oil in a deep pan to medium temperature
4. Fry the bananas slices in batches, until cooked through; avoid burning them
5. Once cooked, spoon out using a slotted spoon into a bowl lined with kitchen towel to absorb excess oil
6. Transfer to a serving dish and sprinkle with salt and toss well.

Sweet Potato Chips (Chips Patat)

Ingredients

- 2 to 3 **sweet potatoes** of different colours
- 500 ml **sunflower oil**

Method

1. Wash the potatoes and pat dry
2. Slice with skin on, into 3mm rings, preferably on a mandolin setting 1
3. Heat the oil in a deep pan to a medium temperature
4. Fry the sliced potatoes in batches until cooked through. Important to watch carefully as they burn easily
5. Once cooked, spoon out using a slotted spoon into a bowl lined with kitchen towel to absorb excess oil
6. Transfer to a serving dish, allow to cool and serve.

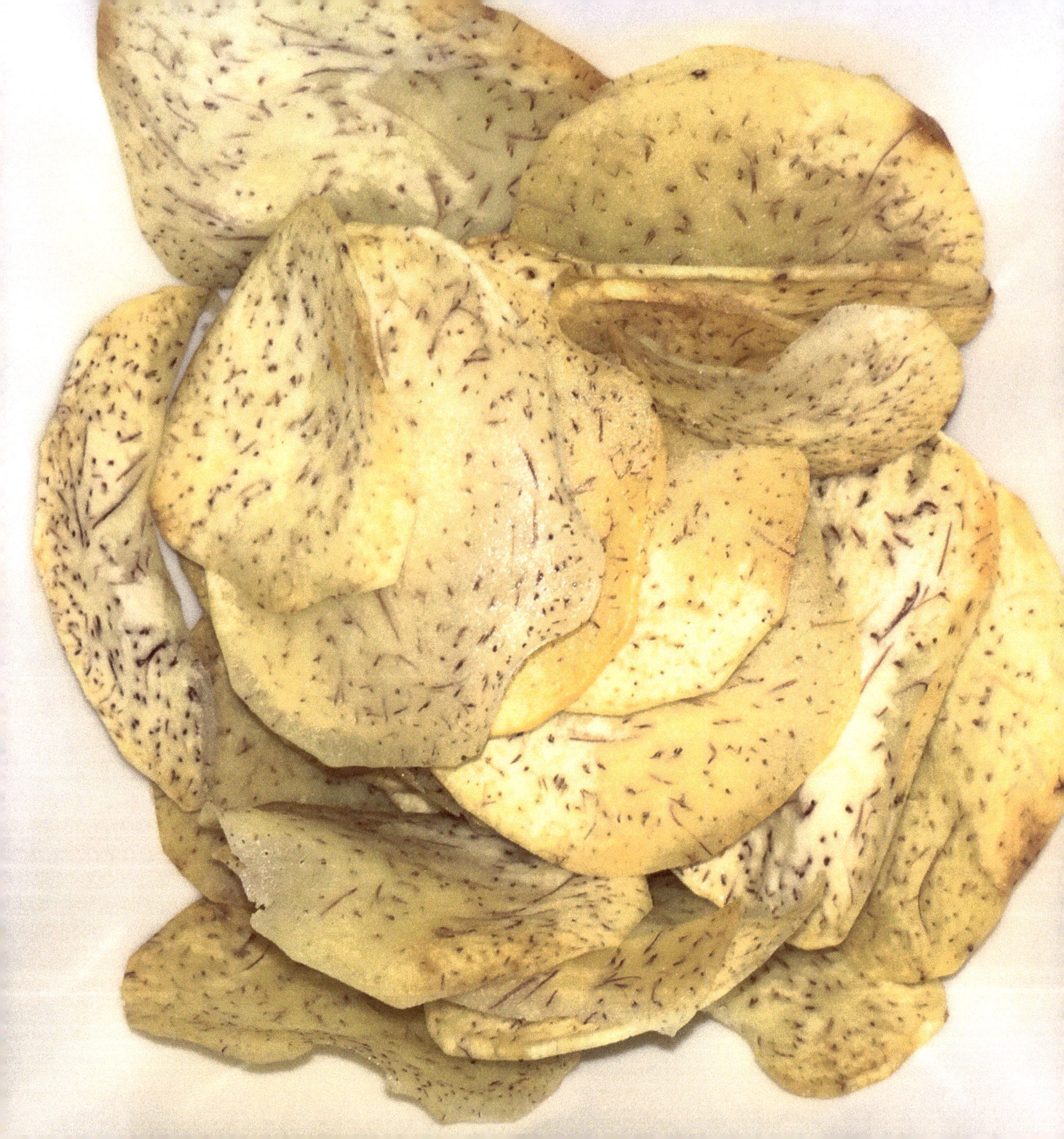

Taro Crisps (Chips Lerouy)

Ingredients

- 2 small **taro** (lerouy)
- 500 ml **sunflower oil**
-

Method

1. Peel the taro and wash well
2. Slice the taro thinly or on mandolin setting 1
3. Wash the taro slices thoroughly in changes of water until the water is clear. This removes the milk which can irritate your throat

137

4. Pat the slices dry
5. Heat the oil in a deep pan to a medium temperature
6. Fry the taro slices in batches until cooked through. Keep a careful watch to avoid burning them
7. Once cooked, spoon out using a slotted spoon into a bowl lined with kitchen towel to absorb excess oil
8. Transfer to a serving dish, allow to cool and serve.

Vegetables Pickle - Asar

Ingredients

- 200 gms **white cabbage**
- 200 gms **carrots**
- One quarter medium **cauliflower**
- 1 small **bitter melon** (margoz)
- 1 medium **brown onion** rougly chopped
- 5 gloves **garlic** grated
- 1 inch **ginger** grated
- 3 **chillies** chopped. Add more to your liking
- 1 heaped teaspoon high quality **turmeric powder**
- 65 ml **brown vinegar**
- 100 ml **sunflower oil**
- 1 tablespoon **oil**

Method

1. Chop cabbage coarsely, julienne the carrots, cut cauliflower in florets and cut the bitter melon in 1 cm squares
2. Bring a pan of water to the boil
3. Blanch the vegetables in the boiling water for 3 to 4 minutes. Ensure they remain crisp
4. Remove from the boiling water and drain well
5. Combine the grated garlic, ginger, turmeric powder and vinegar in a glass bowl. Avoid plastic ones because the turmeric can stain them
6. In a deep pan, heat the oil until very hot
7. Remove the pan from the heat and add the chopped onions and stir well
8. Add the mixture of garlic, ginger, turmeric and vinegar
9. Return to the heat and allow the mixture to come to a boil
10. Add the vegetables, stir for one minute and remove from the heat
11. Stir well and add the chillies
12. Season with salt
13. Allow to cool down before serving or transferring into jars
14. Refrigerate and use at meal-time.

desserts

Banana Fritters

Ingredients

- 3 ripe **bananas**
- 5 tablespoons of **sugar**
- 1.5 cups of **flour**
- 1 **egg** lightly beaten
- 100 ml **milk**
- 1 teaspoon **vanilla essence**
- 2 cups **oil** for deep frying

Method

1. Mash bananas roughly
2. Mix in flour, egg, milk, sugar and vanilla essence
3. Adjust batter if too thick by adding milk. Should fall off spoon easily
4. In a small frypan, bring oil to medium heat
5. Add banana batter by spoonful in the oil
6. Fry until golden brown
7. Remove and place on paper towel on rack or plate
8. Sprinkle with white sugar.

Caramelised Banana
(Bannan Flambé)

Ingredients

- 10 ripe **bananas** – preferably ripe plantain
- 125 grams **sugar**
- 25 grams **butter**
- 100 ml **dark rum**
- 1 teaspoon **vanilla essence**

Method

1. Melt butter in a frypan on medium heat, add sugar and bananas
2. Cook until bananas are caramelised
3. Add the vanilla essence
4. Remove from the heat, add the rum and flame the dish
5. Share the bananas and syrup between 5 dessert plates
6. Top each plate with a scoop of either vanilla (or coconut ice cream for a true tropical taste).

Golden Apple Salad (Hog Plum) – Salad Frisiter

Ingredients

- 8 **golden apples**
- 1 medium size **red onion** finely sliced

Dressing made from;
- 2 tablespoons of **sunflower oil**
- 2 tablespoon diluted **brown vinegar**
- 2 tablespoon **sugar**
- **Salt and pepper**
- Chopped **chillies** (optional)

Method

1. Wash and peel the golden apple
2. Grate using the medium perforation of a grater, discard seeds
3. Place in a large mixing bowl and add the rest of the ingredients and mix thoroughly
4. Adjust for seasoning to desired taste
5. Arrange in a serving dish.

Note: Allow to stand in the fridge for 10 minutes before serving for a refreshing effect.

Green Mango Salad (Salad Mang Ver)

Ingredients

- 4 big green mature **mangoes**
- 1 medium size **red onions** finely sliced

Dressing made from;
- 2 tablespoons of **sunflower oil**
- 2 tablespoon diluted **brown vinegar**
- 2 tablespoon **sugar**
- **Salt and pepper**
- Chopped **chillies** (optional)

147

Method

1. Wash and peel the mangoes
2. Slice to desired thickness using a grater or a potato peeler
3. Place in a large mixing bowl and add the rest of the ingredients and mix thoroughly
4. Adjust for seasoning to desired taste
5. Arrange in a serving dish.

Note: Allow to stand in the fridge for 10 minutes before serving for a refreshing effect.

Pineapple Salad (Salad Zanana)

Ingredients

- 1 ripe **pineapple** (approx. 1 kg)
- 1 medium size **red onions** finely sliced

Dressing made from;
- 2 tablespoons of **sunflower oil**
- 2 tablespoon diluted **brown vinegar**
- 2 tablespoon **sugar**
- **Salt and pepper**
- Chopped **chillies** (optional)

Method

1. Peel the pineapple and remove all the 'eyes'
2. Cut the pineapple in cubes or small wedges
   Do not use the inner core
3. Place the cut pineapple in a large mixing
   bowl and add the rest of the ingredients
   and mix thoroughly
4. Adjust for seasoning to desired taste
5. Arrange in a serving dish

Note: Allow to stand in the fridge for 10 minutes before serving for a refreshing effect.

Salad of Seasonal Tropical Fruits

Ingredients

- 1 medium size ripe but firm **mango**
- 1 small **pawpaw**
- 2 ripe **oranges**
- 2 ripe **bananas**
- ¼ (approx. 250 grams) small **melon**
- 2 **passionfruit**
- 2 **limes** for juice
- 50 grams **sugar**

Hint: You may add any seasonal fruits of your choice but keep to tropical ones.

Method

1. Wash and peel fruits
2. Cut in small cubes and deseed
3. Scoop the flesh from the passion fruit and set aside in a small bowl
4. Squeeze the juice from the limes and set aside in a small bowl
5. Make a dressing from the lime juice, passionfruit flesh and sugar
6. Mix the cut fruits in a salad bowl gently, taking care not to bruise the fruit pieces
7. Pour the dressing over the fruits slowly and evenly
8. Put in the fridge for 10 minutes before serving.

Stews with Coconut Milk (Ladob)

Ingredients

- 1.5 kgs of ripe **plantain bananas** or **sweet potatoes** or **breadfruit** or **yam**
- 4 freshly squeezed **juice from 4 coconuts**
- 250 gms **sugar**
- Pinch of **salt**
- 1 **vanilla pod**
- Pinch grated **nutmeg** (optional)

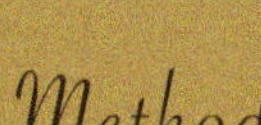
153

Method

1. Wash and peel any of your preferred main ingredient and cut into slices (bananas and breadfruit) and quarters (sweet potatoes and yams)
2. Place the main ingredient in a saucepan and cover with the coconut milk
3. Add the sugar and pinch of salt
4. Cover and cook for 25 to 30 minutes on medium to low heat
5. Slit open the vanilla pod, cut into one inch pieces and add to the pan 10 minutes before the end of cooking time
6. The stew is done when the main ingredient is soft, and the coconut milk has creamed.

Mashed Green Banana with Coconut Milk (Kat-kat Bannan)

Ingredients

- 4 green but mature **plantain bananas**
- 2 milk from 2 freshly grated **coconuts**
- 4 tablespoons of **raw sugar**
- Half teaspoon **salt**
- 1 **vanilla pod** slit open and cut into one- inch pieces

Method

1. Wash and cut the bananas in 3 pieces
2. Boil the bananas with skin on
3. Remove the skin from the boiled bananas and mash with a fork or potato masher
4. Transfer the mashed bananas to a pan and add the coconut milk to it and mix
5. Cook on a medium heat until the cooking milk boils and reduce to a low heat
6. Add the sugar, salt and vanilla pod pieces
7. Stir occasionally to prevent burning at the bottom
8. When the milk has thickened, remove from heat and allow to cool before serving.

It is pleasure that we share with you this collection of recipes of **Seychelles creole cuisine.** Inspired by the growing popularity of our app of the same name, '**Seychelles Creole Cuisine',** and the wishes of users to have it in published form, we hope it does justice to our island nation's diverse origins and reflects the authenticity of our culinary heritage. As with the App, much devotion and passion went into its concept, design, in taking and selecting the photographs featured in the book.

We set out to make to this venture a purely Seychellois one and in this we achieved our objective. From our concept brief, our graphic designer, Olivia Michaud of Angel Creative Design, pulled out all her design skills, meticulously piecing together the pages with excitement and enthusiasm throughout the job. Editing support was provided by Kate Carolus whenever this was needed.

Our team worked diligently and patiently, producing what we believe is a great publication featuring authentic classic creole dishes of the Seychelles. We also claim total ownership of all the photographs contained herein.

Each household has its own method for preparing each dish, reflecting the diverse origins of the Seychellois Creoles, but the result is what matters. The methods used in the recipes featured in this book and our app are based on those of **The Chetty family of Saint Louis,** Mahé, Seychelles. The family, in Seychelles and abroad, lent their unreserved support directly and indirectly during the project, and for this I thank each one of them. But the book would not have been possible without one person whose delicious dishes - prepared from her unwritten large repertoire of recipes - graced the family dinner table each day, while we were growing up. We learnt what great creole cuisine is all about, from **Josephine Lesperance,** the family's live-in house help, originally from La Digue. Her amazing culinary skills produced delectable results each time and this was assured under the watchful eyes of our mother, **Wilhemine Chetty** who had a difficult task. That of pleasing the head of the household, our father **Artoff Chetty.** My siblings, **Chrystold Chetty, Fabiola Horner (Chetty), Lyderic Chetty** and **Gervais Chetty** and **myself** were fierce critics of each dish presented to us and this ensured that the quality was always maintained. Our many friends who came to our house and tasted those exotic dishes never ceased complimenting chef **Josephine.**

To my own household fell the 'enviable' task of tasting the many dishes featured to ensure that they passed the exacting **Chetty family** 'Seychelles creole taste test'. Often, we cooked the dishes a few times until we achieved that perfect harmony of spices, herbs combined with the fresh local ingredients to satisfy the senses of sight, smell and taste.

Thank you to the cohort of judges comprising **Caroline, Stefan, Fabien, Lynn,** and **Michael Chetty** who signed off on every dish and recipe, giving it their highest nod of approval.

Happy cooking and Bon Appetit.

Arnold Chetty Promoter